DIGITAL DAWN: NAVIGATING THE NEW ERA

HARNESSING TECHNOLOGY AND INNOVATION IN THE 21ST CENTURY

DIGITAL DAWN: NAVIGATING THE NEW ERA

IN AN AGE WHERE TECHNOLOGY IS EVOLVING FASTER THAN EVER BEFORE, THE KEY TO SUCCESS IS UNDERSTANDING HOW TO HARNESS IT. "DIGITAL DAWN: NAVIGATING THE NEW ERA" IS A GUIDE FOR THOSE WHO WANT TO STAY UPDATED WITH THE LATEST TECHNOLOGICAL TRENDS AND INNOVATIONS OF THE 21ST CENTURY. IN THIS E-BOOK, YOU WILL DISCOVER: • HOW TECHNOLOGY HAS IMPACTED OUR DAILY LIVES AND BUSINESS. • TOOLS AND STRATEGIES THAT WILL HELP YOU ADAPT TO THE DIGITAL WORLD. • SUCCESS STORIES OF

COMPANIES AND INDIVIDUALS WHO HAVE EFFECTIVELY USED TECHNOLOGY TO ACHIEVE THEIR GOALS. • TIPS ON AVOIDING THE PITFALLS OF OVER-TECHNOLOGIZATION AND MAINTAINING BALANCE IN THE DIGITAL WORLD. WHETHER YOU'RE AN ENTREPRENEUR, A TECH SPECIALIST, OR JUST SOMEONE WHO WANTS TO BETTER UNDERSTAND THE WORLD AROUND US, THIS E-BOOK WILL PROVIDE YOU WITH THE KNOWLEDGE AND TOOLS NECESSARY TO NAVIGATE THE RAPIDLY CHANGING DIGITAL REALITY.

Digital Dawn: Navigating the New Era *Harnessing Technology and Innovation in the 21st Century*

Table of Contents

1. INTRODUCTION

THE DAWN OF THE 21ST CENTURY MARKED A PIVOTAL SHIFT IN HOW WE PERCEIVE AND INTERACT WITH TECHNOLOGY. FROM THE SMARTPHONES IN OUR POCKETS TO THE CLOUD-BASED SYSTEMS POWERING GLOBAL BUSINESSES, THE

DIGITAL REVOLUTION IS BOTH EXCITING AND OVERWHELMING. THIS CHAPTER SETS THE STAGE, PROVIDING A GLIMPSE INTO THE TRANSFORMATIVE POWER OF TECHNOLOGY.

1. Introduction: The Dawn of the Digital Era

As we step into the third decade of the 21st century, we are witnessing an incredible transformation brought about by technology. The dawn of the digital era is not merely a metaphor describing the start of a new day; it's an awakening to a new reality where the boundaries between the physical and digital worlds are increasingly blurred.

A Brief History of Technology

To understand how we got to this point, it's worth looking back. From the earliest computers that occupied entire rooms to portable devices that now fit in our pockets, technology has always been a driving force of progress. In the 1980s and 1990s, desktop computers began to appear in homes, and the Internet became accessible to the masses. In just a few decades, we transitioned from writing letters and mailing them to instant communication via emails, text messages, and social media.

Smartphones: A Revolution in Our Pockets

A pivotal moment in this transformation was the advent of smartphones. These devices, combining the functions of a phone, computer, camera, and many other tools, have become an integral part of our daily lives. They grant us access to endless sources of information, allow us to communicate with people worldwide, and offer apps that make life easier.

Digital Convergence

However, what truly defines the digital dawn is the convergence of technology. Today, we no longer talk about technology as isolated tools or platforms.

Everything is interconnected. The Internet of Things (IoT) allows our devices to communicate with each other, creating integrated systems. Artificial intelligence and machine learning enable computers to anticipate our needs before we even recognize them ourselves.

Challenges and Opportunities

Of course, like any revolution, the digital dawn brings both opportunities and challenges. On one hand, we have access to information and tools that were out of reach for previous generations. On the other, we face challenges related to privacy, security, and the impact of technology on our mental health.

Conclusion

In this chapter, we aimed to provide the reader with a brief overview of the evolution of technology and its influence on our lives. The dawn of the digital era is not just a period of exciting innovations but also a time for reflection on how we want to shape our future in an increasingly digital world.

2. THE IMPACT OF TECHNOLOGY ON DAILY LIFE

OUR DAILY ROUTINES HAVE BEEN SIGNIFICANTLY ALTERED BY TECHNOLOGY. MORNING ALARMS ARE NOW SET ON SMARTPHONES, NEWS IS CONSUMED THROUGH APPS, AND SOCIAL

INTERACTIONS OCCUR IN THE DIGITAL REALM. THIS CHAPTER EXPLORES THE PROFOUND WAYS IN WHICH OUR LIVES HAVE BEEN RESHAPED, EMPHASIZING BOTH THE CONVENIENCES AND CHALLENGES BROUGHT ABOUT BY THESE CHANGES.

2. The Impact of Technology on Daily Life

Technology has not only transformed our workplaces but has also deeply embedded itself in our daily lives. Over the past few decades, it has become so pervasive that it's hard to imagine a day without it.

Daily Routines in the Digital Era

Waking up with a smartphone alarm, checking the weather on an app, communicating with family and friends through social media, ordering food online, or using a meditation app before sleep - these are just a few examples of how technology has become an integral part of our daily routines.

Evolving Consumer Habits

Online stores, streaming platforms, digital subscriptions - our purchasing and consumption habits have undergone a drastic metamorphosis. Thanks to technology, we have access to products and services from around the world with a few clicks or taps.

New Forms of Interaction

Social media, dating apps, virtual meet-ups - technology has not only changed the way we communicate but has also influenced the quality and nature of our relationships. It allows us to stay constantly connected with people worldwide, yet it also challenges us to maintain a balance between our digital and real lives.

Conclusion

In this chapter, we've outlined how technology has become an inseparable part of our daily lives, influencing everything from our routine tasks to the way we communicate and build relationships. While technology offers numerous benefits, it's essential to be aware of its impact and strive for a healthy balance.

3. BUSINESS IN THE DIGITAL AGE

THE BUSINESS LANDSCAPE HAS BEEN REVOLUTIONIZED BY DIGITAL TOOLS AND PLATFORMS. E-COMMERCE HAS OPENED UP GLOBAL MARKETPLACES, WHILE REMOTE WORK TOOLS HAVE

CREATED A DECENTRALIZED WORKFORCE. THIS CHAPTER DELVES INTO THE STRATEGIES BUSINESSES EMPLOY TO THRIVE IN THIS NEW ENVIRONMENT AND THE CHALLENGES THEY FACE IN MAINTAINING A COMPETITIVE EDGE.

3. Business in the Digital Age

The contemporary business world is unrecognizable compared to a few decades ago. Technology has revolutionized not only how companies operate but also how they communicate with customers and the value they offer.

E-commerce: The Global Marketplace at Our Doorstep

E-commerce has transformed local markets into global platforms. Companies that once operated in a single region can now sell products and services to customers worldwide. This has opened doors to new opportunities but also brought new challenges such as international logistics and cultural diversity.

Remote Work: The New Normal

The COVID-19 pandemic accelerated a trend that was already evident: the shift to remote work. Online communication tools like Zoom and Teams became essential, and companies had to adapt to a new work model that's likely here to stay.

Internal Digital Transformation

It's not just about how companies communicate externally, but also how they operate internally. Customer Relationship Management (CRM) systems, business process automation, and data analytics are just some of the tools companies use to optimize their operations.

Conclusion

The digital era has brought a plethora of opportunities for businesses but also many challenges. Companies that can adapt and leverage new tools and strategies stand a chance to succeed in an increasingly competitive environment.

4. TOOLS AND STRATEGIES FOR THE DIGITAL ERA

WITH THE PLETHORA OF DIGITAL TOOLS AVAILABLE, IT'S CRUCIAL TO IDENTIFY THOSE THAT TRULY ADD VALUE. THIS CHAPTER INTRODUCES ESSENTIAL SOFTWARE AND

PLATFORMS FOR
MODERN LIVING,
FROM PRODUCTIVITY
TOOLS TO
CYBERSECURITY
MEASURES, AND
OFFERS GUIDANCE
ON HOW TO PROTECT
ONE'S DIGITAL
IDENTITY IN AN
INCREASINGLY
INTERCONNECTED
WORLD.

4. Tools and Strategies for the Digital Era

In the digital era, where technology is omnipresent, the key to success lies in selecting the right tools and strategies that allow individuals and organizations to achieve their objectives.

Essential Software for Modern Living

Today, we have access to a wide range of software that can facilitate almost every aspect of our lives and work. From project management tools like Trello or Asana to communication apps like Slack or Microsoft Teams. Choosing the right software can significantly boost productivity and efficiency.

Protecting Your Digital Identity

As more of our communication and transactions move to the digital world, safeguarding our digital identity becomes paramount. It's not just about choosing strong passwords. It's also about understanding what information we share online and using tools like two-factor authentication to secure our accounts.

Digital Etiquette and Communication

Communication in the digital realm differs from traditional forms of interaction. Understanding how to effectively communicate via emails, social media, and other digital platforms is key to building strong relationships in both personal and professional life.

Conclusion

The digital era brings a plethora of new tools and strategies that can aid us in achieving success. However, the key lies in understanding how to use them effectively and being aware of potential pitfalls and challenges.

5. SUCCESS STORIES: COMPANIES AND INDIVIDUALS AMIDST THE DIGITAL CHAOS, SOME COMPANIES AND INDIVIDUALS STAND OUT FOR THEIR INNOVATIVE USE OF TECHNOLOGY. THROUGH A SERIES OF CASE STUDIES, THIS CHAPTER HIGHLIGHTS THE

STRATEGIES AND
DECISIONS THAT LED
TO THEIR SUCCESS,
OFFERING
INSPIRATION AND
LESSONS FOR
OTHERS.

5. Success Stories: Companies and Individuals

In the realm of technology and innovation, there's no shortage of inspiring success stories. These tales not only attest to the power and potential of technology but also to human creativity, determination, and vision.

Cases of Companies Leading in Innovation

Some companies have become icons in the digital era due to their innovative solutions. Examples include Apple, which revolutionized the smartphone market, and Amazon, which changed the way we shop online. But it's not just tech giants that have success stories to tell. Many smaller startups have also introduced groundbreaking innovations that deeply impacted their industries.

Individuals Driving Change

Behind every innovative company is a team of people, but often it's individuals who truly push the boundaries and inspire others to think differently. Figures like Elon Musk and Sheryl Sandberg have become renowned for driving change and shaping the future of technology.

Lessons from Success Stories

While every success story is unique, there are common threads and lessons to be gleaned. Innovation, adaptability, understanding customer needs, and a vision for the future are just some of the key elements that recur in many of these tales.

Conclusion

In this chapter, we delved into inspiring success stories in the digital era, looking at both companies and individuals at the forefront of innovation. These stories not only inspire but also provide valuable lessons for those aiming for success in today's tech-driven world.

6. THE PITFALLS OF OVER-TECHNOLOGIZATION

WHILE TECHNOLOGY OFFERS NUMEROUS BENEFITS, THERE'S A DARKER SIDE TO ITS OMNIPRESENCE. THIS CHAPTER DELVES INTO THE MENTAL AND SOCIAL CHALLENGES OF A LIFE CONSTANTLY PLUGGED IN,

DISCUSSING THE IMPORTANCE OF DIGITAL DETOX AND STRATEGIES FOR BALANCING TECH WITH REAL-LIFE INTERACTIONS.

6. The Pitfalls of Over-technologization

While technology has brought numerous benefits to our daily lives and work, there are also challenges and pitfalls associated with its excessive use. In this chapter, we'll explore some of these issues and consider how they can be overcome.

Mental Health Threats

Excessive use of technology, especially social media, has been linked to various mental health issues, such as depression, anxiety, and internet addiction. Comparing oneself to others online, constant information bombardment, and the pressure to always be available can lead to burnout and feelings of overwhelm.

Loss of Privacy

In the digital age, our data is more valuable than ever. However, with every click, share, or online purchase, we expose ourselves to potential privacy breaches. Companies collect and analyze our data, often without our knowledge or consent.

Erosion of Interpersonal Skills

In a world where communication is becoming increasingly digital, there's a risk that traditional interpersonal skills, like face-to-face conversation, might erode. Younger generations, growing up in a screen-dominated environment, might struggle to form deep, authentic relationships in reality.

Conclusion

Technology undoubtedly offers numerous advantages, but it's crucial to be aware of its potential pitfalls. The key is to strike a balance and use technology in a way that enriches our lives rather than dominating them.

7. CONCLUSION AS WE CONTINUE TO SAIL INTO THE DIGITAL FUTURE, IT'S ESSENTIAL TO BE EQUIPPED WITH THE KNOWLEDGE AND TOOLS TO NAVIGATE THE JOURNEY. THIS CONCLUDING CHAPTER REFLECTS ON THE THEMES DISCUSSED AND

OFFERS A ROADMAP
FOR EMBRACING
THE OPPORTUNITIES
AND CHALLENGES
OF THE DIGITAL
AGE.

7. Conclusion: Navigating the Digital Future

As we conclude our journey through various facets of the digital era, it's essential to reflect on what the future might hold and how we can prepare for it.

The Unceasing Evolution of Technology

One thing is certain: technology will continue to evolve. What's innovative today might become obsolete tomorrow. Thus, the key is continuous learning and adapting to new tools, platforms, and trends.

Ethical Challenges of the Digital Era

With technological advancement come new ethical challenges. From privacy and data security issues to artificial intelligence and its impact on society, we need to be aware of these challenges and strive to create technology that serves humanity.

Striking a Balance

While technology offers boundless opportunities, it's crucial to find a balance between the digital and the real. This sometimes means disconnecting, spending time with loved ones, and taking care of our mental and physical health.

Summary

The digital era brings numerous opportunities but also challenges. The key is to prepare for the future, understand the changing technological landscape, and make informed decisions that lead us towards a better future.

SUMMARY AND CONCLUSION

JOURNEYING THROUGH THE PAGES OF THIS E-BOOK, WE EMBARKED ON A CAPTIVATING VOYAGE INTO THE DEPTHS OF THE DIGITAL ERA, EXPLORING ITS VARIOUS FACETS,

FROM DAILY ROUTINES TO GLOBAL BUSINESS CHALLENGES. WE'VE GRASPED HOW TECHNOLOGY HAS IMPACTED OUR LIVES, THE BENEFITS IT HAS BROUGHT, AND THE PITFALLS AND CHALLENGES IT PRESENTS.

IN AN ERA WHERE TECHNOLOGY IS EVOLVING AT A BREAKNECK PACE, THE KEY IS NOT JUST UNDERSTANDING ITS CURRENT CAPABILITIES BUT ALSO ANTICIPATING WHAT THE FUTURE HOLDS. AS EMPHASIZED ACROSS DIFFERENT CHAPTERS, IT'S

VITAL TO REMAIN AGILE, READY TO LEARN, AND ADAPT TO THE EVER-CHANGING LANDSCAPE.

HOWEVER, LIKE ALL JOURNEYS, THIS ONE TOO MUST COME TO AN END. BUT THIS CONCLUSION ISN'T THE END OF OUR CURIOSITY OR OUR

DESIRE TO DELVE FURTHER. ON THE CONTRARY, IT'S MEANT TO SERVE AS A SPRINGBOARD FOR FURTHER EXPLORATION, DEEPER UNDERSTANDING, AND TAKING ACTION IN OUR INCREASINGLY DIGITAL WORLD.

I HOPE THIS E-BOOK
HAS BEEN A SOURCE
OF INSPIRATION AND
KNOWLEDGE FOR
YOU. IF YOU'RE AS
FASCINATED BY THE
DIGITAL ERA AS WE
ARE, THIS IS JUST
THE BEGINNING.
MORE PUBLICATIONS
ARE ON THE
HORIZON, ALLOWING
YOU TO DELVE EVEN
DEEPER INTO THE

MANY ASPECTS OF THIS INCREDIBLE DIGITAL REALM.

THANK YOU FOR JOINING US ON THIS JOURNEY. SEE YOU ON THE PAGES OF THE FUTURE!

www.ingramcontent.com/pod-product-compliance
Lightning Source LLC
La Vergne TN
LVHW041220050326
832903LV00021B/717